Contents

Acknowledgements

The research on children's views described in this report was supported by a grant from the Joseph Rowntree Foundation. It forms part of a larger programme of research on the development of children growing up in different family settings, which is funded by the Medical Research Council.

We are especially grateful to the families who took part for their invaluable help and interest in the study and for their patience in participating.

Thomas G. O'Connor is a key collaborator in this research. We would like to thank Laura Bridges, Lisa Davies, Rowena Dugdale, Jeannine Fraser, Fiona Hollyman, Angela Jones, Gretchen Lussier, K. Pickering and Wendy Sturgess for their participation in the research, and Rebecca Allmark and Francesca Shapland for their help in preparation of this report. We are also very grateful to Susan Taylor, of the Joseph Rowntree Foundation, for her support and advice, and to the members of the Joseph Rowntree Foundation Advisory Group for the study, who gave us constructive help.

Summary

Key findings

Key findings from the project included the following:

- Communication with children about their parents' separation was, for the majority of children in the study, limited. Only 5 per cent of the children reported that they were given full explanation of the separation and opportunities to ask questions. Most of them reported feeling confused and distressed by the situation. Documenting the children's perspective on this issue is an important first step towards testing the relations of these perceived stresses to the children's well-being and adjustment.

- In the first weeks after parental separation, *grandparents* and *friends* were the key intimate confidants; confiding in fathers was rare.

- Children whose parents had experienced more relationship transitions and whose mothers had been pregnant as teenagers described their relationships with both parents as less positive (warm, affectionate, confiding, companionable) than those children whose parents had not had such experiences. Although the children were on average only ten years old, their reports were sensitive to the significance of step and biological relatedness, and of these earlier events in their parents' lives – a striking finding which parallels the patterns of findings from the parents' own accounts of their relationships with their children.

- Children in stepfamilies confided intimately and communicated their problems less with their parents than children in non-step and single-parent families, and less with step-parents than with birth parents. They were less close to their step-parents than to their birth parents, and their 'maps' and drawings of their families echoed this story.

- Children who described relatively high levels of conflict and hostility in their relationships with their fathers and mothers, and greater involvement in parental conflict, had higher levels of adjustment problems than children who described their relationships as low in conflict and hostility. Conclusions about the direction of causal influence should not be drawn from these associations.

- Children's accounts of closeness to their maternal grandparents were related to fewer adjustment problems. There were not significant links with closeness to paternal grandparents. Again, conclusions about the direction of causal influence cannot be drawn. Children's accounts of their closeness to their grandparents did not show high agreement with parents' accounts of the child–grandparent relationship.

- Over half of the children regarded living in two households with some positive feelings, or with no major negative feelings. Positive feelings were associated with being given an active role in decisions about how much time was spent in the two households.

- Children's friendships have been studied relatively rarely in the context of family change, yet the findings on confiding with friends highlight their potential importance as supports. Children with high-quality friendships confided more in their mothers and reported their relationships with their mothers to be very positive. The links were especially clear for children in complex stepfamilies. A key point is that the ability or tendency to confide in peers may be especially unlikely among children with poor parent–child relationships. In high-risk family settings, positive child–mother relationships may be especially important for positive peer relations.

- Children with stepmothers were more likely to confide in friends than children living with their mothers; within stepmother families, negative aspects in the mother–child relationship and involvement in conflict between biological parents were associated with more confiding with friends outside the family.

- Children in single-parent families reported less extensive contact with friends. This was possibly because of relatively fewer resources available to them, or because of their greater involvement in family and household activities. The quality of their friendships was not significantly different from those of children in other family settings.

Practical implications

The practical implications of these findings are as follows.

- It is important for those who care for children to be aware of the extent to which so many children feel that they don't know what is happening in their family world, and may interpret the situation as meaning that they are no longer loved by the parent who is gone.

- Giving children a role in decisions about visiting the second household was helpful in terms of their positive feelings about their divided lives. Helping children to communicate their problems about moving between two households would also be useful.

- As children's friends can be a key source of confiding, the practical implications for parents are that, even if they find talking to their children about the family change very difficult, it may be helpful if they can support their children's friendships.

- The low level of children's confiding in and communication with fathers deserves attention from those who advise/support families.

- The links between the quality of children's relationships with their parents and (maternal) grandparents and their adjustment highlight how important it is to provide support for these relationships where possible.

- The drawings and 'maps' of their families given to us by children as young as four, five and six revealed pictures of their families that in important respects paralleled the accounts given by the older, more articulate children in interviews. The sensitivity of these very young children to the distinction between their relationships with their step-parents and their birth parents, and the significance of their relationships with their grandparents (especially maternal grandparents) were striking. These techniques could be useful clinical tools.

Implications for future research

Clearly, the perspective of children needs to be included in research on families in transition. The findings indicate that through the techniques such as the 'maps' and drawings we can gain a window on the views of children from four upwards concerning their changing family worlds, and that these are messages to which we should listen.

1 Introduction

We first give a brief account of the background to our study, our objectives and the way in which the research was carried out.

Background

By the age of 16, one in eight children in Britain will have experienced parental separation or divorce, and will be living with a new parent as a result of remarriage or cohabitation (Haskey, 1994; Office for National Statistics, 1998). Twenty per cent of children are currently growing up with a single parent (Haskey, 1998), or with a single parent who has a long-term relationship with a partner but does not cohabit. Divorce or parental separation frequently form part of an ongoing process of changes in family relationships (Rodgers and Pryor, 1998). For most children, separation of their parents will involve multiple subsequent family changes, such as living in a single-parent household, new partners for their parents and the experience of living in two households as a result of custody arrangements. These changes in children's lives begin early; most of the children (72 per cent) identified as living in stepfamilies in the Office for National Statistics (ONS) analyses started to do so before they were ten years old.

Children who experience these transitions show higher rates of problems in adjustment than those who have not. The prevalence of such problems (e.g. behaviour and emotional problems, school failure) is on average double that of children in families that have not gone through such transitions (Rodgers and Pryor, 1998). However, these average effects are often *small*, and there is great *variation* between children in their impact (Amato and Keith, 1991). The key questions that need to be answered are the following.

- Which children are particularly vulnerable?

- Which factors in the children's lives act to increase the risk of problems or to protect children?

- What social processes are implicated in these differences?

- What might serve to help children in step- and single-parent families and their parents?

Children's views on relationships, family change and support

Although it is now clear that problems arise for children during these family changes, the emphasis in past research has been on *adults'* accounts of children's difficulties and responses to family transitions. The importance of understanding the perspectives of *children* on their family situations is increasingly stressed by researchers (e.g. Fine *et al.*, 1999), policy makers, those concerned with care and custody arrangements, and clinicians (e.g. Dowling and Gorrell Barnes, 2000), yet we remain relatively ignorant of children's views, especially the perspectives of those in early and middle childhood (Rodgers and Pryor, 1998; for notable exceptions, see Morrow, 1998; Smart *et al.*, 1999). Little is known about whom children see as sources of support, or whom they talk to about their problems.

Recently, there has been a call for greater understanding of social support for children within different types of family as they undergo these transitions (Rogers *et al.*, 1998; Zill, 1994). From late infancy, children closely observe the social relationships of those with whom they are familiar (Dunn, 1993). However, as we have already pointed out, information about children's perspectives on these relationships during family transitions is sparse. In order to fill this gap, a 'whole-family' approach that examines all of the relationships within the family, and includes children's relationships outside the family as well – their friendships and peer relations – is needed. In past research, the emphasis has been on parent–child relationships, with relatively little exploration of relationships with siblings, grandparents and friends. Yet, all of these relationships may well operate as sources of support or stress for children when their family worlds change. Relationships with grandparents, for instance, may well provide support for children (though little information is available on children's own views on these relationships), while relationships with siblings may on the one hand add to children's difficulties, or on the other hand provide comfort and support (Jenkins and Smith, 1990). These patterns may differ in different kinds of family setting; children with step or half siblings have been reported to be more likely to show both long- and short-term problems following family transitions than those in stepfamilies with only biological siblings. It has been proposed that children's relationships with friends and peers are likely to be sources of support during family transitions (Hartup, 1996), but, while this seems a plausible idea, we do not have consistent evidence for or against the notion.

A key goal of our research was to investigate children's views on sources of instrumental and emotional social support at various phases of these family transitions – both their family experiences and their relationships outside the family.

The children in the study

Our study took up an unusual opportunity to conduct an intensive interview study with 192 families, which was framed within a large-scale longitudinal representative community survey of around 9,000 families. Our interview study includes detailed investigations of children's views of their family lives. The study design gave us the advantage of not only having rich information from the children themselves and their parents in the intensive study, but also being able to relate the findings to the large-scale epidemiological study and discover how representative the families were. We could also exploit the archive of longitudinal information on the families over a seven-year period, which was collected as part of the large representative study of 9,000 families.

Objectives

Our aims were to investigate:

- children's views about the changes in their families that occurred during and following parental separation or divorce, and re-partnering

- children's views about their close relationships and support received within these relationships with family members (e.g. biological parents, siblings, resident and non-resident step-parents and stepsiblings, grandparents) and with their friends; and their use of more formal support services (e.g. counselling) during family transitions

- whether children's and parents' views of their family relationships – supportive or difficult – were similar or different

- how far children's views on these close relationships were linked to the number and recent occurrence of these family transitions, and to individual differences in children's adjustment – their social, behavioural, emotional or school problems.

Terms used in the report

Mother: the birth mother of the child, who may be living in the household, or a *non-resident mother* if she is living in a different household from the child.

Father: the birth father of the child, who may be living in the household, or a *non-resident father* if he is living in a different household from the child.

Stepfather/mother: resident parent who is not a birth parent of the child.

Non-step or *intact families*: two-parent families in which the mother and father are biologically related to all of the children in the family, and have not separated or divorced.

Stepfather families: two-parent families in which the mother has children in the household from a previous partnership; there may also be children in the family who are the biological children of the current partnership.

Complex stepfamilies: families in which both mother and partner have brought children from previous relationships; again, there may also be children in the family who are the biological children of the current partnership.

Single-parent families: families in which there is a single parent without a current partner living in the household.

Method in brief

Who took part in our study?

The families we studied in detail in the intensive interview study were recruited from the main large-scale epidemiological community study. We randomly selected 192 families, each with at least two children, from the four family types:

- 50 non-step families
- 48 single-mother families
- 49 stepfather families
- 45 stepmother/complex stepfamilies in which both parents brought children from previous relationships.

The numbers of children studied in these different family settings were 113, 106, 125 and 123 respectively (see Table 1 for details). Of the eligible children, 456 (98 per cent) agreed to participate in the study; of the 11 non-participants, eight were 'visiting' children – that is, whose primary residence was not the household in which our family lived. The proportion of family types is shown in Figure 1 and the ages of the children who were participating are shown in Figure 2.

The large number of five-year-olds (see Figure 2) reflects the fact that all of our families included a child who was participating as a target child in the large, longitudinal study. (Twenty-nine of these target children were four-year-olds who were within three months of their fifth birthday.)

Figure 1 Percentage of families in different family types who took part in the study

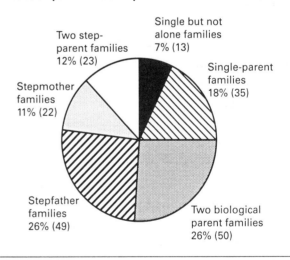

Note: numbers participating are shown in parentheses.

Table 1 The children who took part in the study

	Family type			
	Non-step	Single mother	Stepfather	Complex step
n=	113	106	125	123
Related by birth to both parents	113	0	49	41
Related by birth to mother only	0	106	76	31
Related by birth to father only	0	0	0	51

Figure 2 Ages of participating children

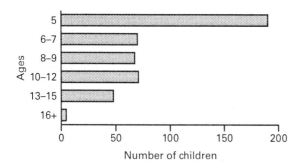

As with other studies of family settings, there were in our group of 192 families significant differences between step, single-parent and non-step families in the prevalence of socio-economic adversities. Single-parent families had significantly lower incomes than other groups, and mothers and fathers in step and single-parent families had experienced more adversities and transitions during their earlier lives than parents in non-step families; these parents were more likely to suffer from depression or malaise (problems in their emotional well-being). The rates of family change (from two-parent to single-parent, from single-parent to stepfamily, etc.) were notably high (see O'Connor et al., 1999 for parallel findings on the full large-scale sample). One implication of these changes is that children who were in single-mother families when we talked to them had frequently also experienced family life with a father present; 80 per cent of children in single-mother families had had a father or stepfather in the household for some period, though, in 17 per cent of cases, the father had left before the child was 18 months old.

How representative of other families were the participating families?

To assess how representative of other stepfamilies or single-parent families the families participating in our interview study were, we compared them with those in the main large-scale representative sample in terms of mother's education, partner's education and weekly family income. For each family type, the families we interviewed did not

differ significantly on these measures from families in the large sample.

In addition, we compared the children participating in our interview study with the children in the large sample on adjustment measures – which give an indication of problems such as difficulties with other children, conduct disorder, aggressive behaviour, worrying, anxious and depressive mood, and withdrawn behaviour – within each of the family types. There were no significant differences in terms of these measures between the children in the interview study and those in the large representative study in each family type.

In summary, the children and their parents in the step- and single-parent families who participated in our interviews were not different from the children and parents in the step- and single-parent families in the large community sample in terms of education, income or children's adjustment.

The interview process

We interviewed separately the children, their siblings, each parent and step-parent, and asked their teachers to complete questionnaires, to get the perspectives of different family members and those who saw the children at school. This report is based on the children's accounts. (For reports drawing on the parents' and teachers' accounts as well as those of the children, see Dunn et al., 2000; O'Connor et al., 2000.)

With the family members, we used informal and more structured interviews, and standard questionnaires. With the younger children (aged four to seven years), we used two more open-ended methods. The children completed a 'map', in which they placed various family members and friends in terms of how close they felt to them; the younger children were also asked to draw their families, and we examined who was left out, and how the family members were grouped in these drawings.

We were able to draw on the information from the main community study on what had happened earlier in the lives of mothers, fathers and children – for instance, the mothers' and fathers' relationship transitions, mothers' teenage pregnancy, the duration of the mother–partner relationship, etc.

What was measured?

In the Appendix, the details of measures and procedures used in the study are reported. The general topics that were assessed included the following.

- *Children's well-being and personal characteristics.* These were assessed in standard measures of adjustment (defined earlier) and assessments of helping, sharing and concern for others (termed 'prosocial behaviour').

- *Children's and parents' accounts of family transitions.* Children and parents were asked about what happened at the time of the parents' separation, with whom they communicated and confided.

- *Children's and parents' accounts of their relationships.* Children, siblings and parents were asked about a wide range of aspects of their relationships with each other and with grandparents. To do this, we used open-ended interviews, standard questionnaires, and the family 'maps' and drawings described above. From the interviews and questionnaires, we derived 'composite' measures of two dimensions of parent–child relationships – the warmth/positive aspects of the relationship, and the critical/hostile/negative aspects of the relationship.

- *Parents' psychological health.* The parents' psychological well-being was assessed using standard self-report measures.

- *Life events.* Children and parents completed reports on the major events – both positive and negative – that they had experienced during their lives.

- *Sociodemographics.* A wide range of measures of education, income, occupation, housing circumstances, neighbourhood, etc. were included.

- *Friendships.* These were assessed with a standard interview focused on qualities of affection, confiding, support, companionship, conflict the child perceived in his/her closest friendship; children were also asked about the number of friends they had, and the frequency of contact with friends.

2 Who is in the family?

In this chapter, we focus on whom children from diverse family settings see as part of their 'family unit'.

Findings from the interviews with older children

From our interviews with children aged between seven and 15, two clear findings stand out: children's views on who were members of their family were linked both to whether they lived in the same household and to whether their parents were their birth parents.

Mothers

Ninety-four per cent of children included their mothers as family members. Those who did not were living in stepmother families (seven) and single-mother families (two). However, 17 children who were interviewed were *not* living with their mothers but with a stepmother, and ten of these did include their birth mothers as family members.

Fathers

Whether the children were living with their father or not made a major difference to whether they included or excluded him from the family unit. All of the children living with their birth fathers included them as part of the family. Of the 111 children who were not living with their fathers, 40 per cent did not include their fathers as a member of their family. There was also a gender effect; girls were significantly more likely than boys to say their non-resident father was not a member of the family.

Resident step-parents as part of the family?

Eighty-four per cent of the children living with a step-parent considered him/her to be part of the family. Those who did not were more likely to come from families with poor income and to have experienced more transitions.

In contrast, children were much less likely to consider their *non-resident* step-parents (the partners of their non-resident biological parents) as part of their families; only 36 per cent were viewed as part of the family.

Perhaps surprising were the findings that children's age, the time that they had spent in the family household, the extent of conflict between their resident parents and the extent of shared family activities – *all of which were important in relation to their adjustment and well-being* – were not related to their views on who was part of the family.

Findings from the younger children's drawings

The children between four and seven years old were asked to draw pictures of their families, and we examined who was included and who was excluded from these pictures; 182 children completed the drawings.

Each child was given a blank sheet of paper titled 'me and my family' and was asked to draw a picture of their family. No further instructions were given and it was left up to the child to decide whom she or he chose to include. When the child was finished, a final prompt was given: 'Are you finished? Anyone else you want to add?' The interviewer asked the child who each figure was and labelled them. From the family tree that was collected as part of the main study, a list of all possible family members was constructed, to which the coder referred in coding inclusion/exclusion. Figures 3, 4 and 5 are examples of drawings from children in different family settings (a complex stepfamily, a stepfather family and a single-parent family respectively).

Key findings from the analysis of who was excluded were as follows:

- Children from step- and single-parent families were more likely to exclude family members than those from non-step families (allowing for differences in family size).

Figure 3 Example of drawings: child in a complex stepfamily

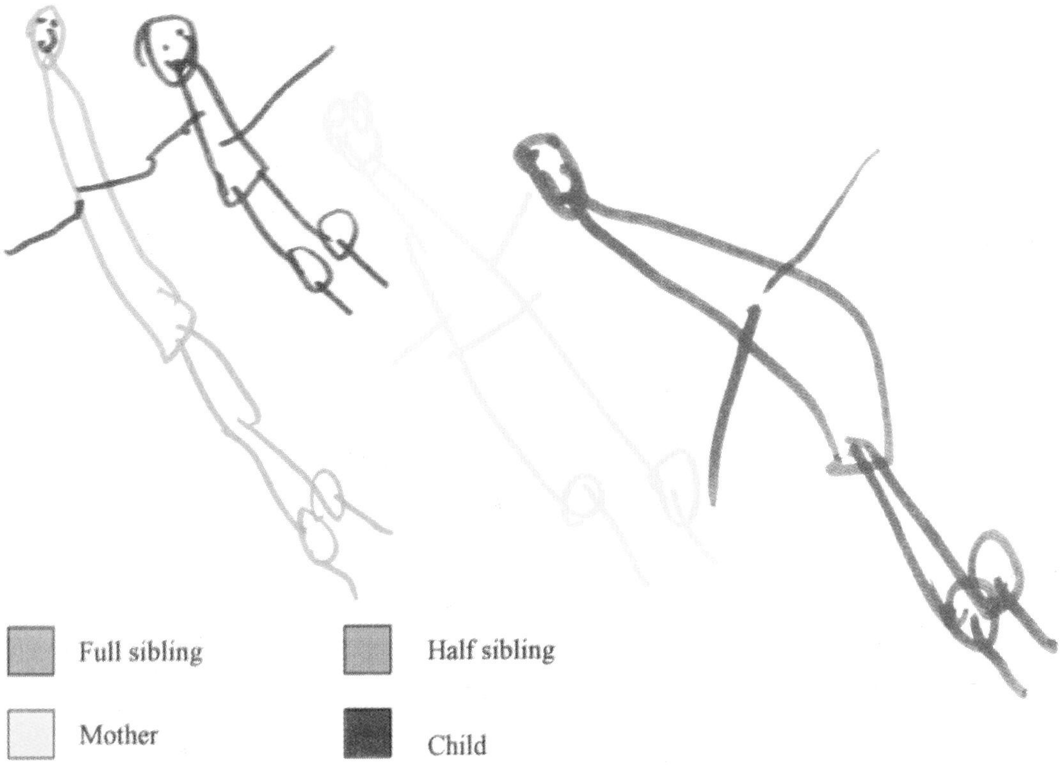

Figure 4 Example of drawings: child in a stepfather family

Figure 5 Example of drawings: child in a single-parent family

Cousin

Self

Grandmother

Mother

Grandfather

Sibling

- Children with both step-parents and birth parents resident in the home were more likely to exclude their step-parents than their birth parents. Thus, in Figure 3, the child has drawn her mother, herself, her full sibling and half sibling, but has left out her stepfather, and her non-resident birth father and his current partner. In Figure 4, the child has drawn herself, her two siblings (one half sibling), her mother, and her non-resident father, but has left out her resident stepfather.

- Step and half siblings were more likely to be left out than full, biological siblings.

- Although, by definition, single mothers did not have a resident partner, often the mother had a current male friend who had frequent contact with the children of the household.

Only one of the ten children in this situation who drew family pictures included the mother's friend in the drawing.

- Some children included grandparents, cousins and other relatives. Thus, in Figure 5, the child from a single-mother family has included her grandparents and cousin.

Summary

The interviews, drawings and maps of their families (see Chapter 4) given to us by the children revealed a notable sensitivity to the distinction between relationships with their birth parents and step-parents; the pictures and maps of the children as young as five and six paralleled the interview accounts of the older children. These techniques could be useful clinical tools.

3 Communication and confiding

It is broadly assumed that it is helpful to children undergoing potentially stressful transitions to have opportunities to talk about what is happening or has happened within their families (Gorell Barnes *et al.*, 1998). Clinical work with children suggests that they often need to be helped to make sense of the changes in their family lives; they need explanations of what has happened and what will happen to enable them to begin to come to terms with it (Dowling and Gorrell Barnes, 2000). Confiding and disclosure have been extensively studied with *adults* undergoing difficult and stressful experiences, and have been shown to be important (e.g. Brown and Harris, 1978). And research with adults who have lived through family transitions in their childhood highlights their recall of the lack of communication with their parents as a key feature of the stress that they experienced (Gorell Barnes *et al.*, 1998; Walczack and Burns, 1984). What about *children's* experiences of communication and confiding? In this chapter, we explore the opportunities they were given to communicate their confusion or feelings about their family situations.

Communication and confiding in the period following parental separation

In our study, we focused on the children who had experienced a family change (that is, we excluded children in step and single-parent families who were born after their parents had separated). Ninety-four children were able to recall the details of the ways they were told about the family change; they were aged on average 10.7 years (SD 2.7), and the separation had happened on average 4.6 years before. (The children who were not able to recall the details of what they were told about the separation were younger – aged on average seven years.)

Figure 6 shows that 23 per cent said no one had talked to them about the change; for 44 per cent it was the mother who had told them, and for 17 per cent it was the mother and father together. In only 8 per cent of cases had the father alone talked to the child about what was going to happen.

In terms of the extent of communication (see Figure 7), 45 per cent of the children reported some communication without explanation, such as blunt statements like 'Daddy's leaving'. Thirty-two per cent reported that they were given some explanation but without details or the opportunity to ask questions; only 5 per cent said that they had been fully informed and encouraged to ask questions.

To whom did the children turn, to talk about these changes in their lives, during the first few weeks after parental separation? We distinguished minor confidences from intimate communication. Figure 8 shows our findings. For intimate confiding, grandparents or other relatives and children's friends were the most frequent confidants, and mothers the next most frequent. Fathers, stepfathers and siblings were rarely confided in intimately; there was one age difference here – older children were more likely to confide in siblings than younger children. Few children

Figure 6 Who told the child about the parental separation?

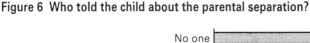
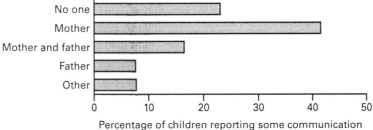

9

Figure 7 Extent of communication at the time of parental separation

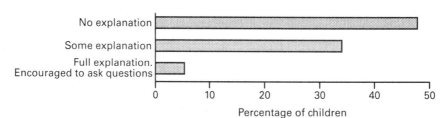

Figure 8 To whom did children confide in the first weeks after parental separation?

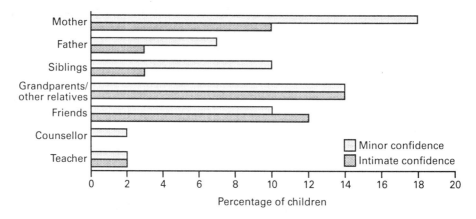

confided in counsellors. So, contact and closeness with grandparents and friends take on particular significance for children faced with family transitions and stress, and we explore these relationships in greater depth in Chapters 5 and 7 of this report.

The poignancy of the children's memories of their experiences at the time of parental separation was striking, as the following examples show.

A seven year old recalled:

Well my Dad went out to work, and he came back later and, er, my Mum had a little go at him and the next morning, well, then my Dad moved out and went with my Nan, and he came back the next morning while we were getting ready for school and he broke the door handle and tried breaking my Mum's arm.

A child of nine described what he remembered of what happened four years earlier:

Nobody told me. I heard. One day we were driving along and we stopped, and we didn't know my Dad

was there, and I opened the door and shouted his name. And he came over and he kneeled down, and Mum told me to shut the door but I didn't want to cos I wanted to be with my Dad. She said 'Shut the door [name]'. And I was only little and I said 'No!' and she said 'Shut the door!' And I said 'No, I don't want to!' so she leant over and slammed the door and we drove off and I saw him out the window just standing there.

A boy of ten recalled that:

We had bunk beds, [younger sibling] was crying in his cot; Dad sat next to me on my bed, and told me. I just sat on my bunk bed and cried.

An eight year old remembered:

I had a funny feeling they were going to split because Mum was always saying to me that Daddy's just sitting around without helping her. We came back from out with our Dad, Mum started shoving him out the door, and our Mum's friend came over, and our Mum shouted at us to get upstairs.

Many children were explicit about the sadness of their feelings about the separation, as the next quotation, from a ten year old, illustrates:

I can't remember the very day but I can remember a couple of weeks later when he came to visit me and I didn't know where he'd gone or anything. So he kept on visiting me and he kept on driving off in the car. I had this rocking horse by the window when I was little, and I used to sit up on the rocking horse and watch his car until I could see it nowhere else, and watch it into the distance. I used to cry my eyes out all night and most of the day. I'd cry and cry and cry.

These accounts highlight the distressing impact of the separation for many children who did not show clinical signs of disturbance.

Current confiding in the family

What about the children's accounts of their *current* opportunities to confide about their problems within the family? These differed with the age of children and, most importantly, with the children's family situation and whether the parent was – in their terms – their 'real' parent or their step-parent. Key findings included the following.

Older children reported confiding with mother and father less than younger children (correlations with age of rs [188] = –.23 and –.22 respectively for mothers and fathers). We therefore took account of the child's age in investigating the associations with the family setting.

Confiding in mothers was less frequent in stepmother and complex stepfamilies than in non-stepfamilies. Confiding in fathers (which was in general less frequent than confiding in mothers) was rarer in stepfather families than in non-step or stepmother families (Figure 9).

But, in general, fathers and especially stepfathers were infrequent confidants when compared with mothers. The following quotation from an eight year old, following the interviewer's question 'Do you talk to [stepfather] about things if you're worried or upset?', illustrates this point: 'No, cos he says I don't care.' A relatively common theme was that fathers and stepfathers *do not understand*, as the next comment from a child about her non-resident father illustrates:

Sometimes I might [talk about my problems] but every time, you know, he might not just understand the things that I'm going through, but if I talk to my Mum, she would understand.

A 12 year old living with her mother put it simply: 'I like my Mum cos I understand her and she understands me.'

Most importantly, the differences in confiding were related to whether the parent was a step-parent or the child's birth parent. Children confided more with both mother and father if they were not step-parents (see Figure 10). And there was more child–father confiding in families in

Figure 9 Current confiding within the family according to family type

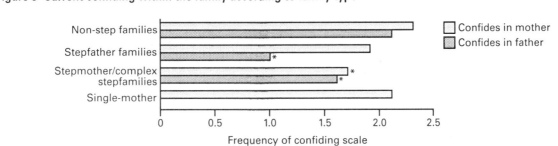

*Significantly different from non-step.

Figure 10 Current confiding within the family according to whether the parent was a step-parent or the child's birth parent

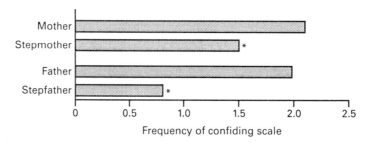

Frequency of confiding scale

*Step relationship shows significantly lower level of confiding than with biological parents.

which there was a stepmother. As one nine year old told us about confiding in the early weeks following the family change:

> The reason I talked to my Dad a lot then was because I didn't feel I could talk to my new Mum at first.

Summary

Communication with children about their parents' separation was, for the majority of children in the study, limited, according to the children. Only 5 per cent reported that they were given a full explanation of the separation and opportunities to ask questions. Most described feeling confused and distressed about the situation. Documenting the children's perspective on this issue is an important first step towards understanding the significance of these perceived stresses for their adjustment.

In the first weeks, grandparents and friends were key confidants; confiding with fathers was rare.

Intimate confiding and communication about problems with parents was less frequent for children in stepfamilies than for those in non-step and single-parent families, and less frequent with step- than with birth parents.

4 Views of family life

In this chapter, we focus on a number of aspects of family life that have been highlighted as key to children's well-being as they face stressful transitions in their familiar worlds.

Children's relationships with their parents

We know from a decade of research that the quality of children's relationships with their parents is of central importance to how they adjust to family changes. As explained briefly in Chapter 1 (and in greater depth in the Appendix), two composite measures were developed from the interview and questionnaire scales: one reflected the positive aspects of the child–parent relationship (warmth, enjoyment of each other's company, etc.) and the other the negative aspects (conflict, feelings of irritability to the other, etc.). In addition to these interview/questionnaire-based measures of the child–parent relationship, we were able to use with the younger children (the four to seven year olds) their four-field maps of how close they felt to family members. In important respects, the interviews and four-field maps told the same story.

Older children
Children from stepmother and complex stepfamilies described their relationships with their (step)mothers as less positive – in terms of the broad set of measures of warmth, intimacy, support, interest and affection we used – than the relationships described by children in stepfather and non-step families (for details of the findings, see the Appendix, Table A1). Children in single-parent families did not differ from those in two-parent (non-step) families in how positive their relationships were with their mothers: they described the affection, support, companionship and shared humour of these relationships in terms that were no different in intensity or warmth from those of children growing up in two-parent families.

In parallel, children in stepfather and complex stepfamilies described their relationships with their stepfathers as less positive than those of children describing their relationships with their birth fathers.

Three points are noteworthy here.

1   In general, there was good agreement between the accounts of children and the accounts of their parents – that is, in families in which the children described a relative lack of warmth and affection between self and parent, the parents were also likely to describe the relationship in those terms (for details, see Dunn *et al.*, 2000).

2   Differences in the extent of the *negative* aspects of the relationship – hostility and conflict – and difficulties in the relationship between child and parent were not on average related to whether the family setting was a step, single-parent, or non-step family. Rather, there were marked differences in the hostility and conflict within child–parent relationships *within each family type*. Both the children's accounts and those of their parents agreed on this point. We examine these issues later in this chapter.

3   The picture from the younger children's four-field maps was similar in some respects to the accounts given by the older children in interviews.

Younger children
Two-hundred-and-fifty-eight children between four and eight years old completed 'maps' of their relationships. We gave each child a blank map with concentric circles and told them that the centre represented themselves; they then completed the map by placing their family members and friends in a series of concentric circles representing the emotional closeness of each relationship. In the outer ring, the child was told to place those with

whom they did not feel close. Each of four domains (family, relatives, school and friends/neighbours) was completed in turn (see Figure 11 for an example).

Where children placed their fathers in the maps varied with both the type of family in which they lived and whether they were stepchildren. Sixty-seven per cent of children living with their birth father placed their father in the central ('really love') circle; in contrast, only 30 per cent of stepchildren placed their resident stepfather in this central circle, which represented feeling emotionally very close (a highly significant difference).

Placement was also linked to stepfamily status: 57 per cent of children in stepfather families placed their resident stepfather in the 'not emotionally close' outer circles, compared with only 29 per cent of children in two-parent, non-step families and 38 per cent of children in stepmother families. These results raised the question of whether, for children in stepfather families, it was family setting or 'step relations' that influenced the children's placement of their fathers. This was investigated by comparing the placement of fathers by the children from stepfather families who were biologically related to the resident father, the stepchildren in these families and children from non-step families.

Figure 12 shows the results, which indicate that it was whether children were stepchildren or living with their birth parents that was key to the placement of fathers as not emotionally close to the children.

Figure 11 An example of a four-field map from a child in a stepfather family

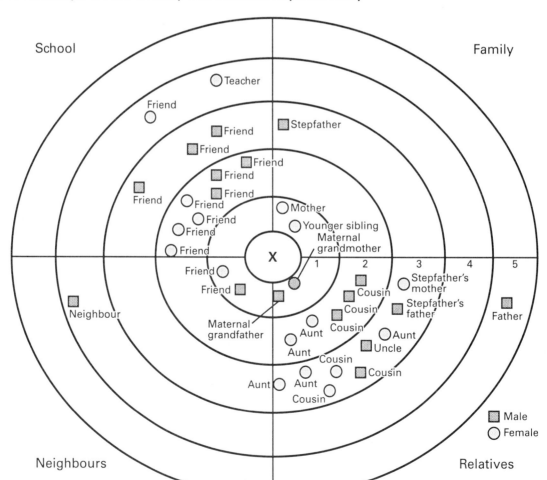

This issue of whether children were stepchildren, or living with their birth parents also affected how children grouped their parents in the family drawings. Those who were related by birth to both resident parents were more likely to group their parents together than the children who had a resident step-parent (see Figure 13).

Children from non-step families were also more likely to draw both parents in the same group as themselves than those from stepfather and complex stepfamilies (Figure 14).

What accounts for individual differences in child–parent relationships?
The central significance of individual differences in the quality of parent–child relationships for children's adjustment has been highlighted in the analyses of the 8,000 children and 4,000 siblings we studied in the large community study (Dunn *et al.*, 1998), as well as in a range of other studies (see Hetherington *et al.*, 1998). Children in the large study who had negative, difficult relationships with their mothers were significantly more likely to

Figure 12 Younger children's views of their closeness to their father

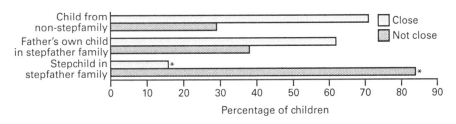

*Significantly different from father's own child in stepfather family.

Figure 13 Number of children who grouped their parents together or separately in the family drawings, according to whether they were stepchildren or living with their birth parents

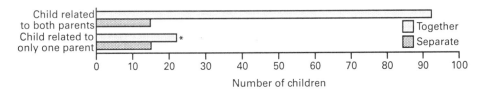

*Significantly different from children biologically related to both parents.

Figure 14 Number of children who drew their parents in the same group as themselves according to family type

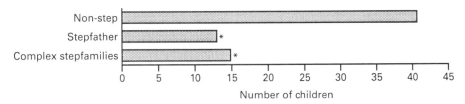

*Significantly different from non-step.

be described by their parents as having adjustment problems (Dunn et al., 1998). So, the issue of what factors contribute to the differences in children's relationships with their mothers and fathers (birth parents and step-parents) is a key one. Although we focus here on the *children's* views of their relationships with their parents, it should be noted that there was in broad terms good agreement between their accounts and those of their parents.

Previous research has suggested the following are likely to be particularly salient factors for parent–child relationships in stepfamilies or single-parent families.

- Parents' own experiences earlier in their lives. For instance, the experiences of girls during adolescence – the age at which they leave home, whether or not they become pregnant as teenagers – have been linked to differences in their parenting (Quinton and Rutter, 1988). We know less about the significance of childhood and adolescent experiences for fathers and for their relationships with their children.

- Social and economic variables, educational level of the parents.

- The mental health of both parents.

- The duration of the current family setting and the number of transitions that family members have experienced.

- The quality of the current relationship between mother and partner, and between mother and ex-partner.

- Whether the child is a stepchild or the parents' own (biological) child and the complexity of the family setting (the presence of children from previous relationships of both parents, for instance).

- Children's own characteristics, including age and gender.

Our analyses then focused on the previous life experiences of both mothers and fathers, and current family factors. We focused on those children over seven years old for whom we had full information from the fathers and mothers as well as from the children, so that we could compare their accounts (106 children in 84 families). The key points from the results were as described below

Child–father relationships

The previous experiences ('life-course' experiences) of both fathers and mothers were important as contributors to differences in how children reported their current relationships with their resident fathers or stepfathers. They described their relationships with their fathers as less positive in those families in which the father had experienced more transitions in his cohabiting relationships. Child–(step)father relationships were also less positive in families in which mothers had experienced teenage pregnancy and several relationship transitions, and in which (step)father and mother had been together for only a short time. These life-course variables together explained 13 per cent of the variance in how positive the relationship was between father and child (see the Appendix, Table A2). When current family factors were added into the analysis (specifically fathers' education, whether father and child were biologically related, family type, and children's age), 37 per cent of the variance in how positive the relationship was between father and child was explained.

Mother's teenage pregnancy and her current emotional well-being also contributed to explaining differences in hostility and negativity in the child–(step)father relationship.

Child–mother relationships

In children's accounts of their relationships with their mothers, again, the previous experiences of the mothers were associated with the marked individual differences in the quality of the relationships. Specifically, in families in which mothers had experienced teenage pregnancies, children reported more negative relationships with their mothers. What was happening currently in the family was also important, and here the mental health of both mother and (step)father, and levels of family income were key. In families with very low income levels, or where the mother or (step)father was depressed, children described their relationships with their mothers in more negative terms.

Sensitivity to parental and step-parental conflict

Conflict between parents who were separated, and between parents and step-parents was reported vividly by several children. They made very clear how much these arguments upset them and how much they themselves were brought into the conflict. As a 16 year old described:

> When he married [stepmother], *it made the whole arguments more heated really. I don't talk to either of my parents about either of them because arguments start and a lot of it gets directed at me, even though it's not really anything to do with me ... they are still arguing with each other through me, which isn't easy or nice.*

Several children commented on how they themselves were the source of disputes between parent and step-parent – as the comments by one ten year old illustrate:

> Once I thought those two were going to split up and it was over an argument about me ... she [mother] *was very upset because she doesn't like it when he* [stepfather] *acts to me and* [sibling] *like we're not his real daughter and son ... he gets all affectionate to* [new half sibling, the stepfather's daughter] *and he totally ignores us.*

One clear message is that parents and step-parents should be aware how much the arguments (let alone the incidents of physical violence) matter to children, and how the fights that children have

witnessed stay with them. One seven year old put it very vividly:

> Everything I see and hear, it just goes inside my head, it's just like a prison in my head, it just shows me pictures and it's like a stereo going round and round, seeing all the things what they said when I was little, so I really know everything because I got a good brain in my head ... They split up because he always used to be horrible to my Mum, chucking her down the stairs and on the bed, and they always used to have fights ... After they split up I was happy because I didn't want to see him because of what he did to my Mum.

One boy, now living with his mother and sister, talked at length about his father's violence to his mother, including the following comment:

> I think at one point I actually saved my Mum's life, I don't know what would have happened, well he was actually trying to snap Mum's back on the settee when I just came screaming down the stairs and then Dad, right, he was really muddled at the time too, so he probably just thought, right oh! Something's wrong here, my child's screaming, so he packed it in, but I don't know what would have happened if he'd carried on and I hadn't screamed.

It was noticeable that some children were extremely sensitive to criticism (both explicit and implicit) by a parent or grandparent of the other parent, and felt that this had very much coloured their views of their other parent. As one seven year old put it, his father 'muddled' him by his criticisms of his mother:

> He was telling me all these stupid things about my mother ... but when grown-ups muddle their children up like that I don't think it's fair cos all he's trying to do is to get me to say that my mother's doing all these awful things to me, and then that would be it, I could go to his house and stay there, but I don't want that to happen, he was muddling me up so much I couldn't stand it.

Children and their non-resident parents

Missing the non-resident parent

Many children expressed clear longing to see more of their non-resident parent. Some expressed wishes that clearly could easily be met, if parents were prepared to do so. For example, one child commented that he wanted to see his father on a weekend rather than a weekday, because they did not get time to talk during the week (school and work demands). Another who had no contact with her father said she'd really like to see him, or to have a picture of him, 'but my Mum doesn't want me to, but I would like to, I would like to.' The younger children often referred to their fathers not seeing them because of work: 'I hardly ever see him because he has to go to work to get money ... I'd like to see him more than I do.'

Many were also aware that their parents did not like them talking about the absent parent; as one nine year old commented: 'Every time I mention Dad, she goes off crying and all that stuff so I can't mention Dad any more.' Another nine year old, living with his mother and siblings, stressed how much he'd like to live with his Dad:

> I never used to disagree with my Mum when my Dad was here but I'm always disagreeing with her now ... If I had a choice I would go with my Dad. I wanna get away from [siblings], they're there all the time.

Visits with the non-resident parent

A repeated theme was the unreliability of the non-resident father; that the child was let down when arrangements for meeting were not kept: 'He says he's picking us up somewhere, but he goes off with his girlfriends.' Again, the practical implications are clear.

Some children made useful suggestions about what would improve their relationships with their non-resident parents; for instance, some commented that they wanted to do things with their non-resident parent on the occasions that they saw them – not simply to sit and watch TV.

Key findings regarding the child–parent relationship

From the analyses of the children's accounts and our studies of the parents' accounts (Dunn *et al.*, 2000), three key findings concerning children's relationships with their parents stand out.

1 *Selective partnerships*. A series of prior events – teenage pregnancy, leaving home early, having a series of cohabiting relationships – increased the likelihood of women forming relationships with men who had also experienced a series of cohabiting relationships and negative life events (echoing the findings from other research on assortative patterns of partner choice in terms of education and depression). The evidence from children and parents is that less affectionate and supportive relationships with both father and mother were the outcome of such selective partnerships. What this means is that children of parents with adverse earlier life experiences were doubly at risk (i.e. from both parents) of less affectionate relationships within the family. The lesson for researchers studying children's outcomes (the way in which children adapt to family change) in different family settings is that information on the prior experiences of both parents can help us understand what contributes to differences in intimate relationships, such as that between parent and child. It is striking that the children's reports were sensitive to the effects of these earlier life-course variables.

2 *Current partner effects*. Our analyses of the parents' own accounts showed, in addition to the 'selection' effects of partner choice that we have just described, that there were more direct influences on parent–child relationships of the way a partner relates to a child. So, for example, the mother's previous life experiences predicted the quality of a

father's or a stepfather's parent–child relationship *even when the father's own earlier life experiences were taken into account and vice versa*. As a second example, the well-being of a father also accounted for differences in a mother's relationship with her child and vice versa. The pattern was evident whichever family member was telling us about the family. Thus, the children's accounts of hostility or critical feelings in relations with their father were linked to their mothers' depression.

3 *Whether child and mother were related by birth, rather than step-relations.* Our findings confirmed the importance of taking account of 'ownness' as distinct from family type. On average, children described significantly more positive relationships with mothers to whom they were biologically related than with stepmothers – a point that is echoed in the findings from the children's drawings and their 'maps' of the family (see above). (Note that there was also evidence from the parents' reports for more problematic relationships among parents and children within the 'complex' stepfamilies; we don't know what exactly the processes that led to these difficulties were, but it seems plausible that levels of stress and tension in the complex stepfamilies might well have contributed to these.)

How children's relationships with their parents were linked to their adjustment

We have stressed that the children's accounts of their distress about their parents' separation are important in their own right – whether or not they are linked to parental or teacher assessments of adjustment problems. However, the question of what links there might be between the children's accounts of their close relationships and family lives remains of course an important one. We investigated these links in the interviews with the children, in their placement of their parents on the four-field maps and in their drawings.

Interview findings

Children's adjustment difficulties were measured using the Child Behavior Checklist (CBCL) (Achenbach, 1991). The externalising scale of this measure includes problems such as conduct disorder, aggressive behaviour, etc. and the internalising scale includes problems such as anxiety and depression. Some of the significant associations with parental assessments of children's adjustment that we found from the interviews with the children from eight to 16 are shown in Figure 15.

Key points include the following:

- Children who reported being involved in conflict between their biological parents were more likely to score high on internalising problems on the CBCL scale.

- Children who reported their relationships with their fathers and their mothers to be very negative were more likely to score high on both internalising and externalising problems on the CBCL scale. Those who reported warm supportive closeness with the mother were less likely to score high on internalising problems.

- Children who reported confiding in their friends were less likely to score high on externalising problems; those who described their friendships as warm, companionate and supportive had lower scores on externalising problems.

- Children who felt positive about life in two households were also less likely to score high on internalising.

Figure 15 Associations with parental assessments of children's adjustment found from interviews with children aged eight to 16

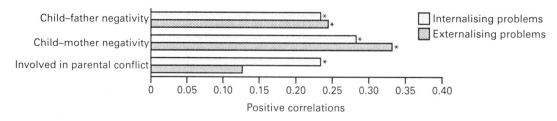

*$p < .05$.

In all of these findings, the direction of effects remains unclear – just as it does in other research on parent–child relationships and adjustment.

The four-field map findings
To what extent were the young children's placement of the resident (step)mother, resident (step)father and siblings on their four-field maps related to their mothers' accounts of their internalising and externalising behaviour (CBCL) and their prosocial (helping, sharing, concern for others) behaviour as measured on Goodman's (1997) Strengths and Difficulties Questionnaire (SDQ)? Our key findings were as follows:

- Children who placed their fathers in the outer circles of the map, reflecting that they did not feel close to them, were almost three times more likely to show externalising problems than children who placed their fathers in the central circle.

- Placement of mothers and siblings was not related to externalising problems.

- Children who placed either their mother or father in the central circles were reported to be more prosocial – that is, more helpful, caring and concerned for others – than those who placed their parents in the outer circles. There were no links between closeness to their resident siblings and their prosocial behaviour.

We next examined, using regression analyses, whether the child's views of his or her closeness to the resident father contributed significantly to their adjustment problems, beyond the other factors that we had already investigated – namely, mother and child relationship transitions, marital status, mother–father conflict, the father's account of his relationship with the child, his educational level, emotional well-being, biological relatedness to child and family income. The results showed that the children's placement of their father on the four-field map made an important additional contribution to explaining individual differences in children's problem behaviour.

Findings from children's drawings of their families
Those children who excluded a family member were reported to have more externalising problems and to be less prosocial, according to their teachers, than children who included all family members.

Shared family activities

Another feature of family life about which we talked to the children was the extent to which they participated in shared family activities – eating meals together, watching TV together, playing games, going out as a family for walks or to visit relatives/ friends. This engagement in shared family events and rituals has been linked in research on adolescents to lower levels of deviance and adjustment problems.

More generally, there is increasing interest in family rituals and cohesiveness as an important influence on children's adjustment, and stepfamilies have been described as less cohesive than non-step families. In our study, it was the children from single-parent families who described the highest level of participation in such shared family activities, while there were no differences between step and non-step families (see Appendix, Table A1).

Lives in two households

Moving between two households on a regular basis is now a common experience for children whose parents have separated. Ninety-eight children in our study moved between two households and gave us their views on living this way. We asked them about sharing rooms, the possibility of different rules being applied in the two homes, whether they had actually had a role in decisions about moving between the homes, and whether they talked to parents in either home about their experiences and feelings about living in two households. Over half the children looked upon living in two households with some positive feelings (some were pleased to get away

from their half or step siblings at the weekend, for instance), or without major negative feelings.

Differences in how children felt about their two-household lives were not related to the kind of stepfamily from which they came, or to their age. But children who had been given an active role in decisions about arrangements regarding time in the two households were more likely to have positive feelings about the two-household life than those who had not. These findings obviously have practical significance.

Children's concerns about other stepfamily issues

The children described their feelings about a range of other aspects of stepfamily life – such as feeling torn loyalty between their biological parents or between their parent and resident step-parent; feeling that they served as a go-between with their separated parents, or between biological and step-parent. The frequency of these responses is shown in Figure 16.

Of particular practical interest are that 30 per cent of step and half siblings reported feeling

Figure 16 Children's concerns about various stepfamily issues

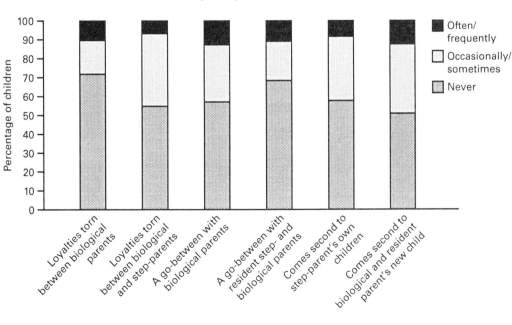

sometimes or frequently upset that they came second to their step-parents' own children. A ten year old commented: 'He treats [own child] more because he's his real child and I'm not.' Another child put his views clearly: 'Well he does treat him better, but I've got my own dad, so I don't care.'

It is notable that 50 per cent of children felt that they came second to the 'new' child of their birth parent and resident step-parent. It is sometimes suggested that the arrival of a baby in a 'reconstituted' family acts as a positive change, increasing family cohesion; in this study, this was not the case for half of the participating children.

Children who had spent time in single-parent families also commented on feeling 'displaced' when their parents formed new relationships. A 12 year old described the changes since she gained a stepfather:

> I always used to look after Mum if she was ill or whatever, but now [stepfather] does that so there's nothing for me to do.

What role should the step-parent have?
A striking feature was the range of differences in how children saw the role of step-parents. Some said step-parents should be friends; as one nine year old put it: 'Like a massive friend, a big friend!'

Others stressed that step-parents should be parents, as the following comments from an 11 year old and a ten year old illustrate:

> I think they should be just like a parent and look after you.

> They should be a parent and care about you, and look after you, and give you treats and that.

Fifty-four per cent of the children thought that step-parents should have the role of parents, 19 per cent thought step-parents should be friends rather than parents and a further 18 per cent thought they should be both friends and parents. The remaining children thought that step-parents should not have the responsibilities of parents nor be considered friends.

It was also evident that, in many stepfamilies, the children resented bitterly the step-parent's attempts to discipline them:

> Cos he's not my Dad.

> He wasn't anything to do with me, so why should he tell me what to do?

> He's got no right to shout at me cos he's not my dad!

Less than half the sample thought that step-parents should have authority in all the usual areas in which parents took responsibility (47 per cent), while 34 per cent thought it appropriate for step-parents to have authority in some areas. Nineteen per cent took the view that step-parents should not have authority over their stepchildren in any issues – within the family or outside it.

In light of the differences in children's perspectives, simple general prescriptions by outsiders concerning the role of step-parents appear inappropriate.

It is worth noting that several of these young children were sensitive to the ways that the stepfather made their mothers happy, as the next two quotations, from nine to ten year olds, illustrate:

> He [stepfather] cheers Mum up when Dad makes her sad.

> At least he makes my Mum happy.

Summary

Children reported less closeness to step- than to birth parents, and their drawings and maps echoed this story.

Those whose parents had experienced more relationship transitions and whose mothers had been pregnant as teenagers described their relationships with both parents as less warm, affectionate, companionable and confiding than those whose parents had not been through such experiences. The children's accounts reflected sensitivity to whether the relationship was a step-relationship, or not, and the links with parental earlier life experiences were paralleled by the parents' own accounts of their relationships with their children.

Children who described their relationships with their parents as high in conflict, criticism and negativity, or who were frequently involved in conflict between their parents, were likely to have higher levels of adjustment problems.

Over half the children who regularly moved between two households reported some positive feelings about living in two households, or no negative feelings. Importantly, the children who said that they had a role in decisions about these living arrangements were more likely to report positive feelings about the two-household life.

5 Grandparents

As we saw in Chapter 3, children cited grandparents as key confidants in the weeks following parental separation. This highlights the significance of understanding the patterns of differences in children's contact and closeness to their grandparents. It is known that grandparent–grandchild relationships can be extremely important to *grandparents;* separation or divorce of parents can be associated with decreased closeness for some grandparent–grandchild relationships (especially paternal grandparents) (Dench *et al.,* 1999; Drew and Smith, 1999) or, for others, increased involvement (Kennedy and Kennedy, 1993). In this chapter, we explore these issues from the *children's* perspective. We examine how children's reports of closeness to and contact with grandparents:

- vary in different types of family and by different patterns of biological relatedness

- are related to the accounts of the grandparent–child relationships given by mothers and fathers

- are related to children's adjustment.

Links between contact with/closeness to grandparents and family setting

Children were asked about the kind and frequency of contact they had with their grandparents, how close they felt to each grandparent and how important this relationship was to them. Both the latter issues were coded on four-point scales ranging from 0 = not at all, to 3 = very close/ relationship extremely important. In terms of contact, it is noteworthy that, in this relatively stable community in the West of England, children reported on average very frequent contact with their grandparents, many of who lived in the same community. Key findings were as follows.

- Contact was greater with maternal than paternal grandparents for all family types, except for children living with a stepmother

and father, who reported less contact with their maternal grandparents. Children in birth mother/stepfather families and children in single-parent families were not significantly different from children living with both birth parents in their rates of contact with their maternal grandmothers or grandfathers – but those living with a stepmother saw their own birth mother's parents less frequently.

- Children living with a stepmother and birth father saw their stepmother's parents (their stepmaternal grandparents) more frequently than they saw the parents of their biological (non-resident) mother.

- Living with a stepfather was associated with lower rates of contact with the child's own 'biological' paternal grandparents. Children living with both birth parents had greater frequency of contact with their paternal grandparents than those in single-mother families.

In terms of the closeness children reported feeling to their grandparents, some key findings were these.

- Children reported greater emotional closeness to maternal grandmothers than to paternal grandmothers, and to maternal grandfathers than to paternal grandfathers. These emotional closeness ratings were not significantly different for maternal grandmothers and grandfathers. Note, in the 'four-field map' shown in Figure 11, the child has placed her maternal grandparents in the closest circle to the centre, but her step-paternal grandparents further out – illustrating this general finding for the sample as a whole.

- Frequency of contact was modestly (but not statistically significantly) linked with children's feelings of emotional closeness to their grandparents.

- Mothers' and fathers' reports of children's closeness to grandparents were strongly linked. Associations with children's accounts were much more modest.

- Only one family type difference was found in parents' reports. Stepmothers reported lower levels of emotional closeness between their stepchildren and the stepchildren's own (biological) maternal grandmothers than the levels reported by mothers in other family settings. These stepmother reports are not consistent with the children's own reports of closeness to their grandparents and suggest that stepmothers may be underestimating the closeness that exists between the stepchildren and their (biological) maternal grandmothers.

How closeness to grandparents relates to children's adjustment

Children's reports of closeness to their maternal grandparents were associated with better adjustment – that is, lower levels of internalising and externalising problems on the CBCL scale. Figure 17 shows the correlations for the full sample; the pattern of associations was similar for each family type considered separately. It was notable that, in stepfather families, there was a stronger link between closeness and adjustment with the *step-paternal* than with the *biological paternal* grandparents. Thus, externalising behaviour problems were significantly lower in children who felt close to their step-paternal grandfather (with a negative correlation of rs = –.57 [p < .01]).

As we have already described, our research showed that events earlier in parents' lives (such as teenage pregnancy and the number of previous relationships) and current family stressors (such as maternal depression and negative feelings in the

Figure 17 How closeness to grandparents was linked with levels of internalising and externalising problems on the CBCL scale

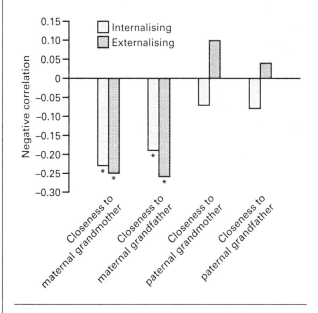

*p < .05.

mother–child relationship) were closely linked to children's adjustment problems. To find out whether emotional closeness to grandparents contributed to differences in children's adjustment beyond the variation explained by other family stressors, we employed regression analyses.

The results showed that emotional closeness to grandparents contributed significantly to lower levels of adjustment difficulties that children experienced beyond the other factors we had already investigated (see Appendix). A similar analysis showed that emotional closeness to maternal grandfathers also made an important contribution.

The main conclusions from these analyses were as follows.

- Family variables accounted for most of the variation between children in their adjustment problems; however emotional closeness to maternal grandparents explained additional variance not accounted for by these family factors.

25

- Emotional closeness to paternal grandparents did not explain additional variance beyond that explained by the other family risk factors.

- When the links between emotional closeness to grandparents and adjustment were investigated separately for each family setting, it was evident that, while the pattern of links described held for the majority of children in the sample (those in non-step families, stepfather families and single-parent families), the patterns of links for children growing up with a stepmother and a biological father were rather different. In these families, greater emotional closeness to the children's maternal grandparents was associated with greater problems in adjustment. For children growing up in stepfather families, it was their emotional closeness to their stepfathers' parents that was linked to adjustment, rather than their relationship with their biological fathers' parents.

In all of these findings, the direction of effects remains unclear. It could be that grandparents feel more warm and affectionate towards their grandchildren *when the children are not difficult or disturbed* (that is, as a consequence of the children's adjustment). Alternatively, or in addition, a close relationship between grandparent and child could exert a protective effect on children who are faced with family problems or transitions.

Summary

Grandparents were key confidants for children over family problems. Children reported greater closeness to their maternal grandparents (both grandmothers and grandfathers) than to their paternal grandparents. Children's emotional closeness to their maternal grandparents was related to fewer adjustment problems – explaining variance beyond that related to other family factors. Children's accounts of their relationship with their grandparents were not closely related to the accounts their parents gave.

6 Siblings

Sibling relationships are potentially powerful sources of comfort, as well as of stress and difficulty for children. This chapter explores whether the children's relationships with their siblings were *different* in families that had undergone transitions. Some studies have reported that conflict between siblings was higher, and sibling support and friendliness lower among siblings in stepfamilies than among those in intact families (Hetherington and Clingempeel, 1992; Hetherington and Stanley-Hagan, 1999; Hetherington *et al.*, 1999; MacKinnon, 1989). Did our study tell a similar story?

Two-hundred-and-seventy-two children aged six years and above reported on their relationships with their siblings. One-hundred-and-ninety-two of these children described their relationship with their five-year-old younger siblings and 80 of these children also reported on their relationship with an older sibling. In these families, the 80 older siblings also described their relationships with their two younger siblings.

How did family setting affect the children's relations with their siblings?

We used information from both open-ended interviews and questionnaires to capture two broad dimensions of the relationships:

1   the affection, sharing of secrets and comforting aspects ('positivity') of the relationship

2   the conflict, teasing, fighting and hostility aspects ('negativity') of the relationship.

Our findings showed family setting *did* affect children's relations with their siblings, although there were some surprises.

- First, the differences between step, single-parent, and non-step families in how the siblings were relating concerned only sibling hostility and conflict. The warmth and emotional closeness between siblings did not differ in the different family settings. This suggests that family transitions have a stronger impact on the levels of conflict between siblings than on the siblings' warmth and closeness to one another.

- Second, the siblings in intact families (i.e. families where the children had not experienced a parental separation) were neither on average the least negative nor the most positive in their relationships.

- Third, children living with single mothers had more conflict and less support in their relationships with siblings than those in other family settings. Figure 18 shows the average levels of negativity in sibling relationships according to family type.

Figure 18 Levels of negativity in sibling relationships according to family type

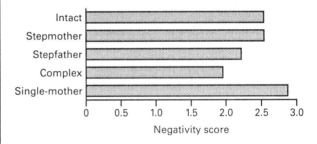

How relationships between step siblings, half siblings and full siblings compare

For most of the sibling pairs that participated in the study, full siblings (i.e. those with the same birth parents) tended to be more negative about each other than half siblings (i.e. those who shared one birth parent). However, there are three caveats to this general story.

- First, the full and half siblings did not differ in the warmth, closeness and companionship they reported in their relations with their siblings.

- Second, differences in negativity between full and half siblings were found for some but not all sibling relationships within any given family. This finding fits with a consistent picture that we are gaining of differences *within* families, in children's adjustment, their behaviour and relationships (see O'Connor *et al.*, in press). The value of studying more than one sibling pair in a family and focusing on individual differences in their relationships, rather than simply investigating average differences by family type and generalising from one sibling pair per family, is brought out here.

- Third, previous research examining differences between full, half and step siblings has shown that the largest difference in sibling relationship quality is between unrelated step siblings (i.e. those who had different birth mothers and fathers) and biologically related siblings (i.e. full or half siblings) (Hetherington and Clingempeel, 1992; Hetherington and Stanley-Hagan, 1999; Hetherington *et al.*, 1999). Because we had relatively few unrelated siblings in our sample, we lacked the statistical power to conduct this comparison. Nonetheless, our results indicated that unrelated siblings were generally the least negative in their relationships, and sometimes the least positive, suggesting that with a larger sample these results would have replicated these previous findings (see Figure 19).

Figure 19 Levels of negativity in sibling relationships according to sibling type

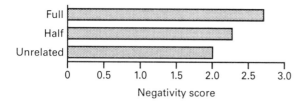

Negativity score

Sibling relationships and children's adjustment

The degree of conflict in the children's sibling relationships was associated with higher levels of behavioural problems, as rated by parents and teachers. For example, externalising problems were correlated with negativity in the sibling relationship at r (80) = .32 for the older siblings' relationship with their five-year-old siblings, and for the middle siblings' relationships with the five-year-olds at r (192) = .20.

We cannot draw causal conclusions from these correlations – it could be that the difficult sibling relationships exacerbated children's behaviour problems, or that children with externalising problems were especially difficult for their siblings to relate to. However, the findings highlight the importance of understanding the variations in sibling relationship quality and their links with children's adaptation and development.

Summary

Family transitions were related to differences in conflict and other negative feelings between siblings, but not to the warm and affectionate aspects of the relationship. The most difficult sibling relationships were reported by children in single-parent families. Within families with three or more children, the quality of the sibling relationships varied markedly. Full siblings tended to be more negative about each other than half- or unrelated siblings.

7 Friends

As we have already seen in Chapter 3, contact and closeness with friends were particularly important for children faced with family transitions and stress. When they were asked to whom they currently confided their concerns or problems regarding family change, 79 per cent of the children replied that it was to a friend, while 20 per cent replied that it was to a relative. This chapter explores this issue further.

What are the links between parent–child relationships and friendship?

The literature on connections between family relationships and friendships is still relatively sparse and inconsistent. We are especially ignorant about what the links may be for children who are faced with family stress or transitions. We investigated three different possibilities concerning these connections between the intimate world of the family and children's relationships with their peers.

1   Are friendships closer among children who enjoy warm positive family relationships – as attachment theorists would predict? Do children who have experienced family problems and parental separation have more conflict in their relationships with other children than those who have not experienced problems within their families?

2   Do children who are faced with difficulties in their relationships at home develop particularly close friendships outside the family?

3   Do children who move between two households, or who come from single-parent homes with restricted resources, have less extensive friendship networks – and thus more constrained opportunities for developing and maintaining friendships?

The children's accounts provided support for each of these ideas for particular family situations (see Dunn *et al.*, 2001, in press for details).

First, the affection and supportive qualities of the children's friendships were positively linked to the confiding, warmth and affection of their relationships with their mothers for the sample as a whole (Figure 20), and for the stepmother/complex stepfamilies and single-parent families considered separately. Of course, we cannot conclude that the quality of their family relationships *caused* poorer or more problematic friendships outside the family – it could well be that characteristics of the children themselves led to difficulties in their relationships both within and outside the family. It was notable, however, that children who were more frequently involved in conflict between their mothers and stepfathers, or who reported problems in communicating with their parents about stepfamily issues, reported less close friendships than other children (Figure 21). The extent of their contact

Figure 20 Positive correlations between family measures and quality of friendship

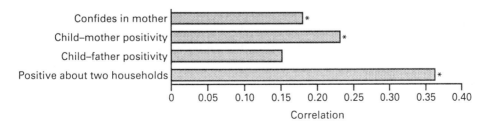

*$p < .05$.

Figure 21 Negative correlations between family measures and quality of friendship

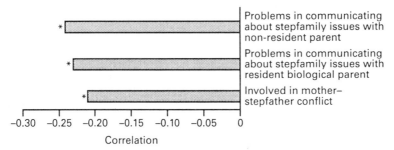

*$p < .05.$

with friends was also greater for children in families in which shared activities were frequent.

There was, however, also some support for the second possibility – that negative aspects of parent–child relationships and conflict within stepfamilies would be associated with closer friendships outside the family. Although children in stepfamilies did not report closer friendships than those in non-step families, the children's comments alerted us to investigate whether step relationships between mother and child, not just family type, were important in relation to friendship. We found that children living with stepmothers had more extensive contact with and confided more in their friends than those who lived with their biological mothers. Whether a child's resident father was a stepfather or a birth father was not associated with differences in the quality of friendships outside the family.

Finally, the idea that friendship networks would be affected by growing up in single-parent households was partially supported: children in single-parent families had less extensive contact with friends, though the quality of their friendships did not differ from those of other children (see Appendix, Table A1).

Findings from the younger children's four-field maps

As has already been described, the children aged between four and seven years in our survey were asked to complete each of four domains (*family,*

relatives, school and *friends/neighbours*) on a map of the closeness of their relationships. The interviewer asked, for instance, 'Who are your friends at school?', then the child chose where to place each person on the map. The child's total emotional closeness score for friends was calculated by multiplying the number of friends in each ring by the score for that ring. We then investigated the association between their emotional closeness to their family members and the number and quality of their friendships.

Key findings (see Sturgess *et al.,* in press for details) were as follows.

- Children who placed their mothers in the central circle had closer relationships with their friends than those who placed their mothers in outer circles. The results here support the interview findings with the older children in the study.

- Children who placed their siblings in the central circle also had closer relationships with their friends than those who placed siblings in the outer circles. These results are of special interest given the sparseness (and inconsistency) of research information on links between sibling and friend relationships (Stocker and Youngblade, 1999). Note that the child whose four-field map is shown in Figure 11 illustrates this pattern of links between both mother and sibling closeness and close friendships: both her mother and younger sibling are in the 'close' circle, and so are two of her friends, a boy and a girl.

- Closeness to fathers was not related to closeness to friends.

As with the findings on adjustment, we cannot draw conclusions about the direction of effects in relation to these family–friend links.

Summary

Friends were reported to be key sources of confiding and communication. Children with close friendships reported close, positive relationships with their mothers. The ability or opportunity to confide in peers may be especially unlikely among children with poor parent–child relationships – that is, in high-risk family settings, positive child–mother relationships may be particularly important for the development of close friendships. Children with stepmothers were more likely to confide in friends than children living with their birth mothers.

Children in single-parent families reported less extensive contact with friends, but the quality of their friendships did not differ from those in other family settings.

Conclusions about direction of effects, between family relationships and friends, cannot be drawn from these correlations.

8 Learning from the children

The vivid and poignant comments made by the children during our conversations with them highlight a range of family issues. What are the practical implications of these for those who care for children?

At the most general level, the importance of *listening* to children faced by family transitions is clear. Overall, the following issues stand out. The first concerns communication – many children felt the changes in their family lives had not been explained to them. They were confused and several interpreted the situation as meaning that they were no longer loved by the parent who had gone. The low level of children's confiding in and communication with their fathers deserves attention from those who advise families. Dowling and Gorrell Barnes (2000) set out for clinicians and parents some guidelines about what information is helpful for children, such as a coherent story about the separation, talk about predictable and reliable practical arrangements (which are kept to), and about what the two homes will mean for the child.

To that list should be added reassurance for children that they will still be able to see their friends, who can be important sources of support – as has been highlighted by this study. For parents, the practical implications are that, even if they find talking to their children about the family change difficult, it may be very useful if they can support their children's friendships.

The children's accounts show us the importance, too, of giving children a role in decisions about visiting their other household, about what their step-parents should be called and about practical aspects of the time children spend with their non-resident parents. The sensitivity of children to the conflicts and distress of their parents is poignantly evident in the study, and carries clear messages to others in their family worlds. Finally, the links between children's adjustment and their perceptions of their relationships with not only their parents but also their maternal grandparents highlight how important it is to provide support for these extended family relationships where possible.

References

Achenbach, T. (1991) *Manual for the Child Behavior Checklist/14–18 and 1991 Profile*. Burlington, VT: University of Vermont Department of Psychiatry

Amato, P.R. and Keith, B. (1991) 'Parental divorce and the well-being of children: a meta-analysis', *Psychological Bulletin*, Vol. 110, pp. 26–46

Brown, G.W. and Harris, T. (1978) *Social Origins of Depression: a Study of Psychiatric Disorder in Women*. London: Tavistock Press

Dench, G., Ogg, J. and Thompson, K. (1999) *The Role of Grandparents*. Ashgate: National Centre for Social Research

Dowling, E. and Gorrell Barnes, G. (2000) *Working with Children and Parents through Separation and Divorce*. London: Macmillan

Drew, L.A. and Smith, P.K. (1999) 'The impact of parental separation/divorce on grandparent–grandchild relationships', *International Journal of Aging and Human Development*, Vol. 48, pp. 191–216

Dunn, J. (1993) *Young Children's Close Relationships: Beyond Attachment, Vol. 4* (1st edition). Newbury Park, CA: Sage Publications

Dunn, J., Davies, L., O'Connor, T. and Sturgess, W. (2000) 'Parents' and partners' lifecourse and family experiences: links with parent–child relationships in different family settings', *Journal of Child Psychology and Psychiatry*, Vol. 41, No. 8, pp. 955–68

Dunn, J., Davies, L.C., O'Connor, T.G. and Sturgess, W. (2001, in press) 'Family lives and friendships: the perspectives of children in step-, single-parent, and non-step families, *Journal of Family Psychology*, Vol. 15

Dunn, J., Deater-Deckard, K., Pickering, K., O'Connor, T., Golding, J. and the ALSPAC Study Team (1998) 'Children's adjustment and pro-social behaviour in step-, single and non-step family settings: findings from a community study', *Journal of Child Psychology and Psychiatry*, Vol. 39, No. 8, pp. 1083–95

Fine, M.A., Coleman, M. and Ganong, L.H. (1999) 'A social constructionist multi-method approach to understanding the stepparent role', in E. Hetherington (ed.) *Coping with Divorce, Single Parenting and Remarriage*, pp. 273–94. Mahwah, NJ: Lawrence Erlbaum Associates

Goodman, R. (1997) 'The Strengths and Difficulties Questionnaire: a research note', *Journal of Child Psychology and Psychiatry*, Vol. 38, pp. 581–6

Goodyer, I.M., Kolvin, L. and Gatzanis, S. (1985) 'Recent undesirable life events and psychiatric disorders of childhood and adolescence', *British Journal of Psychiatry*, Vol. 47, pp. 512–23

Gorell Barnes, G., Thompson, P., Daniel, G. and Burchardt, N. (1998) *Growing up in Stepfamilies*. Oxford: Clarendon Press

Hartup, W.W. (1996) 'The company they keep: friendships and their developmental significance', *Child Development*, Vol. 67, pp. 1–13

Haskey, J. (1994) 'Stepfamilies and stepchildren in Great Britain', *Population Trends*, Vol. 76, pp. 17–27

Haskey, J. (1998) 'One-parent families and their dependent children in Great Britain', *Population Trends*, Vol. 91, pp. 5–14

Hetherington, E.M. (1989) 'Coping with family transitions: winners, losers, and survivors', *Child Development*, Vol. 60, pp. 1–14

Hetherington, E.M. and Clingempeel, W.G. (1992) 'Coping with marital transitions: a family systems approach', *Monographs of the Society for Research in Child Development*, Vol. 57, Nos 2–3, Serial No. 227

Hetherington, E.M. and Stanley-Hagan, M. (1999) 'The adjustment of children with divorced parents: a risk and resiliency perspective', *Journal of Child Psychology and Psychiatry*, Vol. 40, pp. 129–40

Hetherington, E.M., Bridges, M. and Insabella, G.M. (1998) 'What matters? What does not? Five perspectives on the association between marital transitions and children's adjustment', *American Psychologist*, Vol. 53, No. 2, pp. 167–84

Hetherington, E.M., Henderson, S. and Reiss, D. (1999) 'Adolescent siblings in stepfamilies: family functioning and adolescent adjustment', *Monographs of the Society for Research in Child Development*, Vol. 64, No. 4, Serial No. 259

Jenkins, J. and Smith, M.A. (1990) 'Factors protecting children in disharmonious homes: maternal reports', *Journal of the American Academy of Child and Adolescent Psychiatry*, Vol. 29, pp. 60–9

Kennedy, G.E. and Kennedy, C.E. (1993) 'Grandparents: a special resource for children in stepfamilies', *Journal of Divorce and Remarriage*, Vol. 19, pp. 45–68

Locke, H.J. and Wallace, K.M. (1987) 'Marital adjustment test', in N. Fredman and R. Sherman (eds) *Handbook of Measurements for Marriage and Family Therapy*. New York: Bruner/Mazel, Inc., pp. 46–50

Lussier, G., Deater-Deckard, K., Dunn, J. and Davies, L. (submitted) 'Support across two generations: children's closeness to grandparents following parental divorce and remarriage'

MacKinnon, C. (1989) 'An observational investigation of sibling interactions in married and divorced families', *Developmental Psychology*, Vol. 25, pp. 36–44

Morrow, V. (1998) *Understanding Families: Children's Perspectives*. York: JRF/Children's Bureau

O'Connor, T.G., Pickering, K., Dunn, J., Golding, J. and the ALSPAC Study Team (1999) 'Frequency and predictors of relationship dissolution in a community sample in England', *Journal of Family Psychology*, Vol. 13, No. 3, pp. 436–49

O'Connor, T., Dunn, J., Jenkins, J., Pickering, K. and Rasbash, J. (in press) 'Family settings and children's adjustment: differential adjustment within and across families', *British Journal of Psychiatry*

Office for National Statistics (1998) *Marriage and Divorce Statistics 1995*. Series FM2, No. 23, Table 4.4a

Quinton, D. and Rutter, M. (1998) *Parenting Breakdown: the Making and Breaking of Inter Generational Links*. Aldershot: Avebury

Rodgers, B. and Pryor, J. (1998) *Divorce and Separation: the Outcomes for Children*. York: YPS for JRF

Rogers, R.D., Sahakian, B.J., Hodges, J.R., Polkey, C.E., Kennard, C. and Robbins, T.W. (1998) 'Dissociating executive mechanisms of task control following frontal lobe damage and Parkinson's disease', *Brain*, Vol. 121, pp. 815–42

Rutter, M., Graham, P. and Yule, W. (1970) *A Neuropsychiatric Study of Childhood*. London: Heinemann

Smart, C., Wade, A. and Neale, B. (1999) 'Objects of concern? – children and divorce', *Child and Family Law Quarterly*, Vol. 11, No. 4, pp. 1–12

Stocker, C.M. and Youngblade, L.M. (1999) 'Marital conflict and parental hostility: links with children's sibling and peer relationships', *Journal of Family Psychology*, Vol. 13, No. 4, pp. 598–609

Sturgess, W., Dunn, J. and Davies, L. (in press) 'Young children's perceptions of their relationships with family and friends: links with family setting and adjustment', *International Journal of Behavioral Development*

Walczack, Y. and Burns, S. (1984) *Divorce: the Children's Point of View*. London: Harper & Row

Zill, N. (1994) 'Understanding why children in stepfamilies have more learning and behavior problems than children in nuclear families', in A. Booth and J. Dunn (eds), *Stepfamilies: Who Benefits? Who Does Not?*, pp. 97–106. Hillsdale, NJ: Erlbaum

Appendix

Methods and measures used in the study

Procedures

Home visits were made to each family participating. Mothers/stepmothers, fathers/stepfathers and children over the age of seven were each interviewed individually in a room on their own, and completed questionnaires. Children between the ages of four and seven completed drawings and family 'maps'. Teachers were mailed questionnaires. This report is based on the children's perspectives on their experiences and relationships; parent and teacher data are not discussed here (see Dunn *et al.*, 2000 for a description of findings on parent information on parent–child relationships, grandparent–child relationships, and for further details of methods and measures).

Measures

Children's well-being and personal characteristics

Children's adjustment difficulties were measured using the Child Behavior Checklist (CBCL) (Achenbach, 1991). The externalising scale of this measure is the sum of items such as conduct disorder, aggressive behaviour, etc.; the internalising scale is the sum of items such as withdrawn, anxious, depression and somatic complaints.

Children's prosocial behaviour (helping, sharing, concern for others) was measured with the Prosocial Scale of Goodman's (1997) Strengths and Difficulties Questionnaire (SDQ).

Gender, age, and temperamental characteristics were included in the measurements.

Parents' and children's accounts of number of transitions

The number of changes in live-in or married relationships that the parents had experienced and the children had lived through.

Children's and parents' views of their relationships

Composite scales of the positive and negative dimensions of child–parent relationships were formed from the following.

1   Interviews in which children and parents individually reported on their warmth, wish to spend time together, enjoyment of the other's company, confiding, noticing when the other was upset, action when the other was upset, their enjoyment of spending time with the other (positive aspects of the relationship). They also reported on their critical/irritable feelings towards the other, the frequency of conflicts between them, the intensity and the degree of upset both child and partner experienced, the frequency of physical conflict (negative aspects of the relationship).

2   Questionnaires covering expressive and instrumental affection, discipline and conflict.

Details of the scales, their origins, reliability and psychometric properties are given in Dunn *et al.* (2000).

Parents' well-being and psychological health

Marital status (married, cohabiting, single); *parent age; education; biological relatedness to child; parental malaise* (an assessment of emotional wellbeing – Rutter *et al.*, 1970); *marital happiness and conflict* – a composite score was formed from scores on three scales: the Family Conflict Inventory (Hetherington, 1989), and two scales from the Locke-Wallace Marital Adjustment Test (Locke and Wallace, 1987).

Life events

For both mothers and their partners, the following variables from their childhood and adolescence were included:

- *parental divorce* – those whose parents were divorced before the children were 18 were distinguished from those who had not

- *teenage pregnancy* – information collected during mothers' pregnancy.

Life Events, a semi-structured interview developed by Goodyer *et al.* (1985), was employed. This covers events in the following categories: accidents, deaths, illnesses, legal, marital, family, parental separation/divorce, disasters, school, in which the negative impact is rated and only events that carry moderate to severe negative impact are included.

The *duration of current mother–partner* relationship was also coded.

Sociodemographics

Information on *income, occupation of mother and partner, housing circumstances* (including crowding), *perception of financial stress* was included in the main community study.

Friendships

The quality of children's friendship was assessed with a standard interview (see Dunn *et al.*, 2001, in press).

Closeness to grandparents and children's adjustment

The contribution of child-reported grandparent closeness to the explanation of individual differences in children's externalising problems beyond the variance explained by other family variables was investigated with regression analyses (for details, see Lussier *et al.*, submitted). Variables entered in the first step of the regression models were number of mothers' relationship transitions, maternal depression and mother–child negativity. For maternal grandmothers, these variables accounted for a significant proportion of the variance in externalising problems ($F (3,113) = 24.18, p < .01$; R squared = .39). Addition of the children's closeness to their maternal grandmothers

Table A1 Mean differences (standard deviation) in children's reports on family and friendship measures by family type

| | Family type | | | | F (df) |
	Non-step	Stepfather	Stepmother/ complex	Single-parent	Adjusted for age
Confides in mother	2.30 (0.72)	1.88 (0.98)	1.69 (1.08) [a]	2.11 (0.81)	(3,228) = 4.68**
Confides in father	2.08 (1.05)	1.02 (1.02) [a]	1.61 (1.09) [b]		(2,180) =15.19**
Family activities	2.69 (0.66)	2.86 (0.65)	2.71 (0.75)	3.26 (0.66)	(3,184) = 6.37**
Child–mother positivity	0.22 (0.75)	0.02 (0.70)	−0.38 (0.94)[ab]	0.19 (0.71)	(3,186) = 5.87**
Child–mother negativity	−0.22 (0.85)	0.07 (0.89)	0.05 (0.87)	−0.03 (0.75)	(3,185) = 0.98
Child–father positivity	0.39 (0.61)	−0.16 (0.74) [a]	−0.06 (0.99)		(2,105) = 4.18 *
Child–father negativity	0.02 (0.71)	0.07 (0.86)	0.15 (0.78)		(2,104) = 0.23
Contact with friends	–	0.11 (0.67)	0.10 (0.61)	−0.33 (0.67) [c]	(2,179) = 7.93 *
Quality of friendship	3.92 (0.50)	3.85 (0.65)	3.89 (0.70)	3.83 (0.82)	(3,187) = 0.13

Note: – Question not asked.
$*p < .05. **p< .001.$
[a]Significantly different from non-step families.
[b]Stepmother/complex families significantly different from stepfather families.
[c]Single-parent families significantly different from stepfather and stepmother families.

to the model resulted in an increase in the explained variance (F (4,112) = 19.64, $p < .01$; R squared = .41). This increase was statistically significant (F change = 4.07, $p < .05$).

The same approach was used to examine the possibility that closeness to maternal grandfathers also contributed to the variance in children's externalising problems, beyond the contribution of other family variables. As with the findings for maternal grandmothers, the regression models showed that the addition of closeness to maternal grandfathers to the models explained a statistically significant increase in variance of externalising behaviour. Thus, family variables accounted for the majority of the explained variance in children's externalising problems, but closeness to maternal grandparents explained additional variance not accounted for by other family variables.

Table A2 Regression analyses of child report of father–child positivity: life-course and current family variables

	Model 1			Model 2		
	Coefficient	(SE)	t	Coefficient	(SE)	t
Life-course variables						
Father transitions	−0.31	(0.17)	−1.81	−0.33	(0.18)	−1.80
Mother transitions	−0.41	(0.17)	−2.76*	−0.16	(0.25)	−0.66
Teenage pregnancy	−0.25	(0.18)	−1.37	−0.19	(0.17)	−1.11
Time in relationship	−0.11	(0.26)	−10.43	−0.18	(0.22)	0.83
Current family variables						
Father education (1) vs. (2)				0.04	(0.15)	−0.27
Father education (1) vs. (3)				−0.55	(0.21)	−2.57*
Father biological				−0.59	(0.24)	−2.40*
Family type (1) vs. (2)				0.36	(0.30)	1.19
Family type (2) vs. (3)				0.39	(0.25)	1.61
Child age				−0.11	(0.03)	3.63*

Model 1: $R^2 = 0.13$; F (4,83) = 4.53*.
Model 2: $R^2 = 0.37$; F (10,83) = 7.69*.
* $p < .05$.